A Beginner's Guide To
Doberman Pinschers

Written By
Bernadette E. Winkler

Contents

© 1986 by T.F.H. Publications, Inc. Distributed in the UNITED STATES by T.F.H. Publications, Inc., 211 West Sylvania Avenue, Neptune City, NJ 07753; in CANADA by H & L Pet Supplies Inc., 27 Kingston Crescent, Kitchener, Ontario N2B 2T6; Rolf C. Hagen Ltd., 3225 Sartelon Street, Montreal 382 Quebec; in CANADA to the Book Trade by Macmillan of Canada (A Division of Canada Publishing Corporation), 164 Commander Boulevard, Agincourt, Ontario M1S 3C7; in ENGLAND by T.F.H. Publications Limited, 4 Kier Park, Ascot, Berkshire SL5 7DS; in AUSTRALIA AND THE SOUTH PACIFIC by T.F.H. (Australia) Pty. Ltd., Box 149, Brookvale 2100 N.S.W., Australia; in NEW ZEALAND by Ross Haines & Son, Ltd., 18 Monmouth Street, Grey Lynn, Auckland 2 New Zealand; in SINGAPORE AND MALAYSIA by MPH Distributors (S) Pte., Ltd., 601 Sims Drive, #03/07/21, Singapore 1438; in the PHILIPPINES by Bio-Research, 5 Lippay Street, San Lorenzo Village, Makati Rizal; in SOUTH AFRICA by Multipet Pty. Ltd., 30 Turners Avenue, Durban 4001. Published by T.F.H. Publications, Inc. Manufactured in the United States of America by T.F.H. Publications, Inc.

1.
Introduction

Just watch the eyes of onlookers as you walk your Doberman; watch the heads turn! Who wouldn't be captivated by the lithe lines of power, the natural athletic grace, the alert and vital look, and the proud, aristocratic spirit of your Dobe!

Contrary to Doberman Pinschers' unjustified reputation as dangerous dogs, they are by nature friendly and intelligent. Photo by Vince Serbin.

All dogs have a keen sense of smell. Nevertheless a Doberman intended to perform police work must be trained to discriminate specific scents. Photo by Sally Anne Thompson.

Your dog is truly special. His breed is registered by the American Kennel Club; his recorded history goes back to the last decade of the nineteenth century. He was originally bred as a working dog, and he is used throughout the world for performing various public duties: police work, guard work, rescue work, seeing-eye work—these are some of his more common jobs. He is an extremely useful dog because he has a keen intelligence; he is a rapid student. He is very affectionate and obedient, and he has boundless energy. Blue ribbons are mere child's play for your Dobe—he has been cited for his heroic rescue work in the army, and quite a few pet Dobes have played major roles in saving the lives of children in danger.

All of this, however, is little more than legend compared to the unsung joys of the Doberman as a family pet! Your Dobe could hardly be such an intelligent student and such a devoted worker if he did not have such a large and loving heart! Devotion is his best characteristic. He is a one-family dog and would rather starve than switch loyalties.

Facing page: *Note the sharply defined rust markings required by the standard in show Doberman Pinschers. Photo by Isabelle Francaise.*

The impressive appearance of a Doberman in the backyard is enough to make potential intruders think twice before stepping onto your property. Photo by Sally Anne Thompson.

With small children your Dobe is as gentle as a mother; with young boys he is a rollicking pal, with masters of households he is an indispensable ally, and with mistresses of households he is a wonderful pet. But woe to the uninvited intruder, to the malicious trespasser or the thief. For your Dobe's heart is solely with the family hearth, nor can it be bribed or cajoled! His affection is unswerving and rooted deeply in the family to which he belongs

2.
Origins

The Doberman Pinscher, a relatively new breed, first gained notice in Germany in the 1880's; yet his origins remain somewhat of a mystery. In those days it was not uncommon to find unique types of dogs developed through inbreeding in localities isolated because of slow transportation means.

The profile is seriously considered in judging a show Doberman. The top of the skull must be flat, never domed or rounded. Photo by Vince Serbin.

A Doberman that was trained for guard duty will perform unerringly when necessary. However, a dog that shows aggressive behavior in the show ring can be dismissed by the judge. Photo by Sally Anne Thompson.

The original home of the Doberman probably was a small German town in the province of Thuringia called Apolda. It is claimed that a dog warden, Louis Dobermann, bred a "smart" dog to aid him in his duties. The Old German Shepherd was one of the dogs Dobermann apparently used, though this is not certain. Dogs such as the Weimaraner and the Rottweiler (German working dog) are believed to have contributed to the Doberman's stock. Such a fine dog as the Doberman is sure to have many breeds claiming precedence in producing his distinct characteristics. It may indeed be true that the German Shepherd, the Great Dane, the Dachshund, and the French Bloodhound known as the Beuceron contributed to the eventual breed of the Doberman as we know him today. Only one thing regarding the Doberman's origins is clear, the importance of the role that Herr Dobermann played in developing the breed. We can thus state with some certainty that the Doberman Pinscher originated in the province of Thuringia, sometime in the later 1800s. The word *pinscher* in German means "terrier", so the name Doberman Pinscher actually means Doberman Terrier.

However difficult it is to pinpoint the exact origins of the Doberman, no one can doubt the actual existence of this noble breed. A man from Apolda named Otto Goeller was so eager to develop the better qualities of the Doberman that his kennels soon became crowded with fine specimens of our dog—much to the dismay of his neighbors, who complained of the noise. Goeller had to reduce the number of dogs he kept, but the size of his enthusiasm was not daunted, and he went on to found the first *Dobermannpinscherklub* in Apolda in 1899. The breed was soon officially recognized in Germany. Goeller is the first important breeder of Dobermans as show and pet rather than guard dog. He was influential in developing a uniform type and standard of usefulness and beauty which acted as solid foundation for later breeders. Clearly Herr Goeller was not concerned over how much Rottweiler or Dachshund or Great Dane or Weimaraner blood flowed in the Doberman's veins—he was interested in the Doberman Pinscher as a special breed.

Almost as soon as the Doberman Pinscher was recognized in Germany in 1900, he became a popular show dog. During the first ten years of our dog's popularity in Germany a number of illustrious champions were bred, and today most Dobermans throughout the world have some of these German ancestors in their pedigrees.

It was not long before the Doberman's popularity became worldwide. In 1902 the first club for Doberman Pinschers in Switzerland was formed. In that country a few mishandled and rowdy dogs gave the Doberman a bad name, but responsible breeding and ownership of Dobermans has brought about a chance in the Swiss attitude. Now the Swiss enjoy the Doberman's spirit and utility. By 1909 Dobermans had reached Holland and even the Dutch East Indies. Soon other countries such as England, Austria, France, Belgium and Italy boasted of Doberman Pinscher clubs.

Most dogs were originally bred for usefulness, and the Doberman is no exception. Today he is one of the best watchdogs and guard dogs to be found, and he is renowned for his work in various K-9 corps. The British used Dobermans in both World Wars. The Germans had 6,000 dogs in the service in 1914, and a large number of these were Dobermans. And most of us associate the fame of the Doberman with his service in the U.S. Armed Forces in the Second World War.

The K-9 Corps of the U.S. Marines often used Dobes for scouting purposes. The Marines and their dogs spearheaded the attack in the

A Doberman Pinscher is an obedient dog and will obey his owner's command to "sit." Photo by Vince Serbin.

Dogs and bitches vary in height, ideally; female Dobermans are shorter then males. Photo by Vince Serbin.

South Pacific, and several Dobermans were cited for their work.

In one case a Doberman's keen senses of hearing and scent proved infinitely better than radar. Carefully trained to silence and stealth, he led his master through dense jungle, and when his ears and nose warned him of an enemy gun nest in the vicinity, a barely audible growl would begin to rumble in his throat and chest, so quietly his master would have to feel his throat for vibrations. Then, after a hand signal from his master, he would stop growling. Thus one by one the gun nests were located and pinpointed. In a similar way other Dobermans gave warning of Japanese snipers and located their position. Alert and loyal, fearless and well-disciplined, the Doberman Pinscher helped save the lives of many of our American sons in the Philippines.

The breed of the Doberman Pinscher was officially recognized in America in 1908, which means that the Dobe must have been known on our continent even before that date. Some important early breeders were Mr. and Mrs. Herman Meyer of Philadelphia, Mr. and Mrs. Vocassovitch of Boston, and Mr. Jaeger of Rochester, whose kennels came to be known among dog fanciers throughout the nation. In 1922 the Doberman Pinscher Club of America was founded.

In 1923, Peter Umlauff, a renowned Doberman Pinscher authority, was invited to judge Doberman entries. In the Westminster Dog Show (the "major league" of America's dog shows) of 1923, the importance of German blood in American Dobermans was obvious. The most outstanding dogs in that show were offspring of German champions such as Alto v. Sigalsburg and Helios v. Siegestor.

Many German champions were imported into the United States in the earlier 1900s, thus giving the Doberman a good footing in the States insofar as breeding is concerned. So it was not long before American breeders of Dobermans began producing champions. The Pontchartrain Kennels and the Glenhugel Kennels have produced American champions.

Probably the most perfect Doberman ever bred was American. Ch. Rancho Dobe's Storm was without precedence in winning Best-in-Show at the Westminster Dog Show twice in a row. Although the Germans have never bred as fine a dog as Storm, it is often felt that German Dobermans are, on the average, of a slightly higher quality that American Dobermans. Other American champions of importance are Ch. Dictator v. Glenhugel and Ch. Delegate v. d. Elbe. Ch. Dortmund Delly's Colonel Jet and Ch. Brown's Eric are famous sires, while famous dams of champions are Ch. Jessy v. d. Sonnenhoehe and Meadowmist Isis of Ahrtal.

The highlights of the Doberman's history are so captivating that they sometimes have an unfortunate effect—some people never realize the dog has a large, affectionate heart. By nature he is a warm and loyal dog who prefers to be a peaceful pet and not a war hero or public guardian.

3.
Purchasing

If you are planning to purchase your Doberman from a pet shop, a kennel, or a private party, it would be wise to keep a few things in mind. First and foremost, choose a dog that appears to be sound and healthy—symptoms of poor health are usually obvious. To

A good breeder can be judged by the appearance of the kennel he maintains. Photo by Vince Serbin.

make sure that the puppy you buy is healthy, take him to a registered veterinarian immediately. Most reputable dealers in dogs will suggest that you do this, anyway. The vet will give you a certificate of health for your puppy and this should be assurance enough. If, for any reason, your pup should not receive the certificate, the dealer should accept the returned pup. It would be an excellent idea for you to make an agreement to this effect with the dealer before visiting the vet. It is better to buy a Doberman puppy than an adult because the puppy is not attached to anyone when you get him and because a puppy is easier to train. The Dobe tends to be a one-man or one-family dog, and he does not easily switch his allegiance.

Deciding whether you want a male or a female may be difficult. Each sex has advantages. The female is generally regarded as the better family pet because she tends to be gentler and less adventuresome. She is easier to train, more affectionate and faithful, and, of course, she can have puppies. The male, on the other hand, is lacking in none of these qualities except the last, and his greater strength and spirit often win the day.

Because your Doberman is an uncommon and rather special dog, you will want to know what distinguishes him. Your Doberman is fairly large, he is muscular and powerful, and he will need plenty of room to run in. He will be happiest in a suburb, in a city park, or out in the country. He carries himself with alert and proud elegance, reflecting a fine nobility that makes him outstanding. He has great endurance and speed. He is short-haired and thus easy to wash and groom. His color may be black, brown, or blue, all with tan trimming. His tail is cropped short and his ears are usually trimmed to stand up.

Show-winning Dobermans are those which come closest to the standards set by the standard-approving dog association in your country. Because standards vary from time to time and place to place check with your national association to obtain the current standard.

General conformation and appearance: The *appearance* is that of a dog of good middle size, with a body that is square, the height, measured vertically from the ground to the highest point of the withers, equaling the length, measured horizontally, from the forechest to the rear projection of the upper thigh. Height, at the with-

A magnificent Doberman Pinscher owned by William A. MacKay. Photo by Isabelle Francais.

In the United States, the cropping of a Doberman Pinscher's ears is commonly practiced, except where it is not traditionally accepted or prohibited by law. Photo by Vince Serbin.

ers, males 26 to 28 inches, ideal being about 27 inches; bitches, 24 to 26 inches, ideal being about 25½ inches. Compactly built, muscular and powerful, for great endurance and speed. Elegant in appearance, of proud carriage, reflecting great nobility and temperament. Energetic, watchful, determined, alert, fearless, loyal, and obedient. *Faults:* Coarseness. Fine Greyhound build. Undersized or oversized. *Disqualifying faults:* Shyness, viciousness. *Shyness:* A dog shall be judged fundamentally shy if, refusing to stand for examination, it shrinks away from the judge; if it fears an approach from the rear; if it shies at sudden and unusual noises, to a marked degree. *Viciousness:* A dog that attacks, or attempts to attack, either the judge or its handler is definitely vicious. An aggressive or belligerent attitude towards other dogs shall not be deemed viciousness.

Head (shape, eyes, teeth, ears). *Shape:* Long and dry, resembling a blunt wedge, both frontal and profile views. When seen from the front, the head widens gradually toward the base of the ears in a practically unbroken line. Top of skull flat, turning with slight stop to bridge of muzzle, with muzzle line extending parallel to the top line of the skull. Cheeks flat and muscular. Lips lying close to jaws,

20

and not drooping. Jaws full and powerful, well filled under the eyes. Nose, solid black in black dogs, dark brown in brown ones, and dark gray in blue ones. *Faults:* Head out of balance in proportion to body. Ram's, dishfaced, cheeky, or snipy heads.

Eyes: Almond-shaped, *not* round, moderately deep set, *not* prominent, with vigorous, energetic expression. Iris of uniform color, ranging from medium to darkest brown in black dogs, the darker shade being the more desirable. In reds or blues, the color of the iris should blend with that of the markings, but not be of a lighter hue than that of the markings. *Faults:* Slit eyes. Glassy eyes.

Teeth: Strongly developed and white. Lower incisors upright and touching inside of upper incisors—a true scissors bite. Forty-two teeth (22 in lower jaw, 20 in upper jaw). Distemper teeth should not be penalized. *Disqualifying faults:* Overshot more than 3/16 of an inch. Undershot more than 1/8 of an inch.

Ears: Well trimmed and carried erect. (In all states where ear trimming is prohibited, or where dogs with cropped ears cannot be

This is an adult Doberman Pinscher whose ears are uncropped.

shown, the foregoing requirements are waived.) The upper attachment of the ear, when held erect, should be on a level with the top of the skull.

Neck: Carried upright, well muscled and dry. Well arched, and with nape of neck widening gradually toward body. Length of neck proportioned to body and head.

Body: *Back* short, firm, of sufficient width, and muscular at the loin extending in a straight line from withers to the slightly rounded croup. *Withers* pronounced and forming the highest point of body. *Brisket* full and broad, reaching deep to the elbow. *Chest* broad, and *forechest* well defined.

Spring of ribs pronounced. *Belly* well tucked up, extending in a curved line from chest. *Loins* wide and muscled. *Hips* broad in proportion to body, breadth of hips being approximately breadth of body at rib spring. *Tail*, docked at approximately second joint, should appear to be the continuation of the spine, without material drop.

Forequarters: *Shoulder blade and upper arm* should meet at an angle of 90 degrees. Relative length of shoulder and upper arm should

Where ear trimming is allowed, the ears are trimmed surgically by a veterinarian and then supported by a splint. Photo by Vince Serbin.

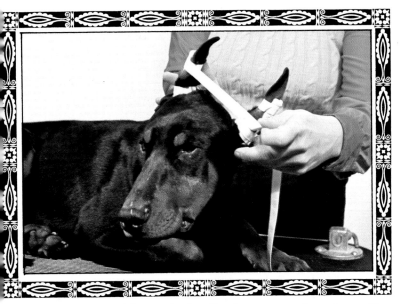

To guarantee an upright growth, the splinted ears are taped together, as illustrated here. Photo by Vince Serbin.

be as one to one, excess length of upper arm being much less undesirable than excess length of shoulder blade. *Legs*, seen from the front and side, perfectly straight and parallel to each other from elbow to pastern; muscled and sinewy, with round, heavy bone. In a normal position, and when gaiting, the elbow should lie close to the brisket. *Pasterns* firm, with an almost perpendicular position to the ground. *Feet* well arched, compact, and catlike, turning neither in nor out.

Hindquarters: In balance with forequarters. *Upper shanks* long, wide and well muscled on both sides of thigh, with clearly defined stifle. *Hocks* while the dog is at rest: hock to heel should be perpendicular to the ground. *Upper shanks, lower shanks,* and *hocks* parallel to each other, and wide enough apart to fit in with a properly built body. The *hipbone* should fall away from the spinal column at an angle of about 30 degrees. The *upper shank* should be at right angles to the hip bone. Croup well filled out. *Cat-feet*, as on front legs, turning neither in nor out.

Gait: The *gait* should be free, balanced, and vigorous, with good reach in the forequarters and good driving power in the hindquarters. When trotting, there should be a strong rear action drive, with rotary motion of hindquarters. Each rear leg should move in line with the foreleg on the same side. Rear and front legs should be thrown neither in nor out. Back should remain strong, firm and level.

Coat, color, markings: *Coat*, smooth-haired, short, hard, thick, and close-lying. Invisible gray undercoat on neck permissible. Allowed *colors*, black, brown, or blue. *Markings*, rust red, sharply defined, and appearing above each eye, and on muzzle, throat, and forechest, and on all legs and feet, and below tail. White on chest, not exceeding one-half square inch, permissible.

The foregoing description is that of the ideal Doberman Pinscher. Any deviation from the above-described dog must be penalized in proportion to the extent of the deviation, and in accordance with the appended scale of points.

Disqualifications

Shyness, viciousness. Overshot more than $\frac{3}{16}$ of an inch; undershot more than $\frac{1}{8}$ of an inch.

Barring certain obvious faults, there is no way of predicting the future show value of a puppy, but an intelligent guess can be made on the basis of the quality of his parents.

If you are careful, the Doberman you bring home will be healthy, noble and attractive—and who knows, perhaps inherent in your devoted pet is a champion.

4
The Puppy

Your puppy's pedigree and his application for or certificate of registration, which you should have received upon purchase, are two completely different things. The pedigree is simply your puppy's ancestral chart. The certificate or application form is an important piece of paper: it is a means to the official registration of your

Directly striking your Doberman puppy during training is not necessary. Instead, you must show your displeasure by action or voice. Photo by Sally Anne Thompson.

puppy. If you have a registration certificate then the breeder from whom you bought your puppy has already named him and registered him with the American Kennel Club; in this case you must file a transfer and send it, with the proper fee, to the American Kennel Club, 51 Madison Avenue, New York 10010, NY. Soon you will receive a new certificate. If, on the other hand, you have received the application form, simply fill it out (don't forget to name your pup) and send it to the AKC, enclosing a fee.

The first nights

Your pup's first night in his new home will not be easy for him no matter how brave he may be. Remember, it is his first night away from his family and his new home is still strange to him. He even had to leave his habits behind, for the most part. His mind will be in a swirl of confusion for awhile. So, make things easy for him.

He will probably enjoy his first day home as an adventure, but adventures are fatiguing. By nighttime your puppy's excitement will have changed to yawns. It is common for young puppies to whine, occasionally, during their first night home. Try not to let this bother you.

It is best to let him adjust to his new home before showing him off to neighbors, and take special care when children are around. Small children don't know the difference between a toy dog and a live one and their play is sometimes rough. Why take a chance of creating hard feelings between your Doberman and them? Ask the children to be gentle, and they'll understand.

A place to sleep

You may decide to make a doghouse for your puppy, or you may decide to let him sleep in your home. The Doberman adult is well suited to chilly weather in spite of his short hair. A very small puppy, however, whether it is a Doberman or any other breed, should not be thrust out into the cold of winter nights. So it is best, if you plan to bed your Doberman in a doghouse, try to buy your puppy in the warmer months so that he may gradually become accustomed to the harshness of winter. If you have bought your puppy during the winter months, you will have to help him make the adjustment. When it is below freezing, let him play outside a great deal, but let him sleep inside—a heated garage would serve admirably. When it is above freezing, his doghouse is the place for him, provided you have supplied it with bedding. When he is five or six months old, he should have no trouble sleeping in his doghouse every night.

The doghouse: The doghouse should be well constructed. Its floor should be slightly above the ground so that it will not get wet, and its roof should be slanted and leakproof to keep out the rain. The door should be just large enough for the grown dog, but no larger. A larger door invites drafts. A burlap or canvas curtain hung over the inside of the door will discourage drafts. For the same reason the sides of the doghouse should be well sealed against wind and rain. You should furnish the doghouse with some sort of bedding—an old blanket or rug will do well.

If your dog is to sleep indoors, find a place for him that is not in a draft, yet is not too near the heat. A warm and dry cellar or garage is an ideal location for your puppy's bed and eating facilities.

Feeding

Prepared dog foods, such as kibble or meal, are excellent staples for the feeding schedule you will plan for your puppy. Of course you will supplement his basic meal with meats, fat, vitamin-mineral supplements and table scraps.

It is best to keep your puppy to a firm feeding schedule. When he is three months old he will need three meals a day; at six months of age, two meals a day will be sufficient.

For the young puppy, the morning meal will consist of one cup of prepared dog food. The noon meal will consist of a cup of warm milk and dog biscuits or kibble, and the evening meal will consist of about a half a cup of prepared dog food, some meat, a few tablespoons of fat drippings and perhaps some table scraps.

After he is six months old, you will need to feed your puppy only twice a day, giving him two or three cups of prepared dog food in the morning (depending on how hungry he is) and one cup of prepared meal supplemented by table scraps, meat, fat drippings and a boiled egg in the evening. After he is a year old he will probably need 4 or 5 cups of prepared meal and 1 cup or two of meat per day, to be fed mostly in the evening.

A commercially prepared vitamin and mineral powder should be included with the dog's food, following the directions contained thereon. It is a good idea also for growth and coat to add recommended amounts of cod-liver oil and wheat-germ oil several times weekly.

If you wish to allow your puppy to feed himself instead of giving him regular meals, simply put the required amount of food in his dish and let him eat at will. If he finishes the whole dish before the day is over, do not refill it. Soon you will be able to fill his feeding dish with a great deal of kibble, and he will not overeat.

Most people already know that it is dangerous to feed either puppies or grown dogs chicken or fish unless it has been carefully deboned. The small sharp bones may get stuck in his throat. A large beef bone, however, will not only be well-received by your puppy, but it will help him through his teething periods; and a bone is certainly better than a table leg or your new shoes. Nylabone is highly recommended by veterinarians as a safe, healthy nylon bone that can't splinter or chip. Instead, Nylabone is frizzled by the dog's chewing action, creating a toothbrush-like surface that cleanses the teeth and massages the gums. Nylabone and Nylaball, the only chew products made of flavor-impregnated solid nylon, are available in your local pet shop. Adding a tablespoon of fat drippings to your puppy's meal will help him develop a fine, shiny coat. Avoid giving him starchy foods.

You should keep in mind the fact that your puppy is an individual with individual needs. For example, he may grow tired of one kind of food. Be flexible with your menu and quantities. Remember that no strict system of rules will work for every dog. You will find that common sense is the best guide.

Housebreaking

You should start to housebreak your puppy as soon as you get him, but do not expect the best results for awhile. Remember he is still young. Before he was weaned, he needed the help of his mother to excrete. His muscles were not developed well enough to enable him

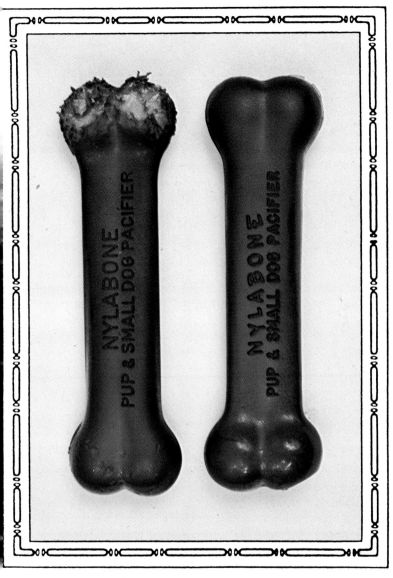

One of these Nylabones is badly chewed up. However, it is perfectly safe for your pet at all times. Photo by Vince Serbin.

to perform this necessary function by himself. The muscles in a puppy's excretory system are just beginning to work shortly before he is weaned. He is not able to control these muscles until he is several months old. So you will probably not gain much headway in this housebreaking training at the beginning. But there is no harm in letting him know what is expected of him.

Before you begin to house-train your puppy, it would be wise to set down a few rules which form the basis of training. Do not be an overbearing dictator. Through fear a dog learns only to be vicious, and this may spoil him for human contact. Your puppy is extremely intelligent; he is full of love for you, and it will be painful enough for him to be reprimanded by a sharp and firm voice. A sharp word while he is doing the wrong thing will be quite effective, but don't stop here. Pick him up and put him on some newspapers, or whatever facilities you may have devised, and when he gets the right idea, praise him and love him. Some people feel that rewarding him with food is a good practice because it accomplishes the desired end. But it is far wiser to reward him with love and pat him, for this will help create the relationship you will want.

You can reduce your training problems a great deal by confining your puppy to one or two rooms of the house, where you can keep your eye on him much of the time. If he is used to newspapers, keep some clean ones on the floor at all times. When he starts to show signs of needing to excrete (such as putting his nose to the floor and circling around in search of a likely spot), take him to his appointed toilet and hope that you can prevent an accident. It is helpful to keep one soiled newspaper on the floor in the beginning of his house-training period, because dogs like to do their duty in places that have been used before. A commercially prepared housebreaking aid is available at most pet shops. This will aid in getting your dog to go to this one predetermined spot for this purpose. If you are fortunate to have caught him in time, praise him and pat him. This is the right way to teach him.

You will find that he will not be difficult to housebreak, for he is naturally clean, just as his mother was. Nonetheless, if you have a young pup, be prepared to clean many a mess. Even the process of cleaning your puppy's messes will help him learn the right way to adjust to living inside. You should clean very thoroughly, using a little vinegar or bleach in your water. This eliminates the faintest traces of an odor which might encourage your puppy to repeat his mistake.

Some people like to combine paper training with outdoor training. Simply follow the same basic techniques outlined for indoor house-training, except take your puppy outside as often as convenient. You will find that as your puppy grows older his self-control will increase.

Early training

You will find that "Come" is among the easiest commands for your puppy to learn. Because he has a great deal of love for you he naturally will wish to be near you, so it does not require much coaxing to make him come. However, he should learn to come on command. Then, you will be able to protect him from dangerous situations such as busy streets.

Always use a very simple word or hand signal, and try not to use a similar-sounding word for two different commands. Your dog will

Experience proves that cats and dogs, even Dobermans, can coexist in the same habitation. Photo by Vince Serbin.

Regular brushing keeps the Doberman's coat shiny and healthy. Dead skin and loose hair are removed along with dust and grime. Photo by Sally Anne Thompson.

have difficult distinguishing between words that sound alike, such as "run" and "come." Your puppy should not be forced to come. If you force him, he will learn to associate something unpleasant with the command word, and this is the last thing you want.

Call him to dinner or play with a clear "come". When he responds properly, you should reward him with a pat. Repeat this several times a day, but do not expend much time in any one session.

Occasionally you may encourage him to obey with a bit of food, but it is best not to make a habit out of this practice. After your puppy has begun to learn the simple "Come" command, you may wish to add his name to it. You will find this helpful, for it will serve to get your puppy's attention.

Your puppy's vet

If you don't already know of a good veterinarian ask the person from whom you obtained your puppy, ask the man in your pet shop, or ask your neighbors and friends who have pets. These people have a certain amount of experience. If all else fails, call the Humane Society in your neighborhood.

Once you have chosen a good vet for your puppy you will want to take your pet to see him as soon as possible. He needs protection against two common diseases, distemper and infectious hepatitis. Fortunately your vet can immunize your puppy against these two puppy illnesses. At this time he will also give your puppy a general checkup. It may be that the previous owner had a temporary serum administered. This serum is effective for about two weeks. These days, however, a permanent vaccine may safely be administered at a young age. At any rate before taking your puppy home you should check with the previous owner about shots.

You should check with the previous owner to find out when your puppy was last wormed. Discover if he needs reworming and, if so, when. If everything appears all right, don't hesitate to check your puppy's stool for long white worms, particularly if he seems listless. If your puppy has worms discuss the matter with your vet who will recommend proper treatment.

Don't be afraid to consult your vet for any advice regarding your pup. Don't be afraid to go along with his suggestions either. Remember that he has had years of training and experience.

Several types of dog brushes are available. It is best to get a well constructed brush with firm bristles.

A Doberman puppy intended for conformation competition must learn the pre-scribed show stance as early as possible. Photo by Sally Anne Thompson.

5
First Aid

cannot be emphasized too strongly that proper care is essential to ~~o~~ur puppy's health. Here are some first aid hints.

~~a~~ny time your puppy becomes chilled or wet, take him to warmth ~~an~~d shelter and dry him off. His natural way of drying off by shak-~~in~~g is not adequate for cold weather.

flea spray can contain powerful chemicals. Manufacturers recommend use *~~onl~~y in areas of good ventilation. Photo by Sally Anne Thompson.*

Try not to let your puppy become exposed to extreme changes in temperature. Like humans, he is susceptible to colds and chills.

Have a dog sweater available for very cold days.

If your dog is constipated, a couple of teaspoonfuls of castor-oil will rapidly remedy the situation. Constipation may be the sign of improper feeding. Cut down on his milk and increase his water, vegetables, and add roughage in the form of dog biscuits. The opposite problem—loose bowels—is also usually a sign of improper feeding. Kaopectate, skim milk, and cereal of oats and corn should bring your dog back to normal. If not, call your vet.

When your dog is sick, don't punish him for breaking housebreaking training. Remember, he is not well. Comfort him.

For minor ear ailments, a commercially prepared medicated ear wash is available in most pet shops. Used as directed, this is quite helpful.

There is a kind of bug which is particularly fond of dogs—the flea. He can be an irksome pest, but he can easily be banned from your home and your puppy's coat. If you see your dog scratching persistently, you need not search his coat with a magnifying glass—you can assume that a family of fleas is living on your dog. In this case, a bath with commercial flea soap followed by an ample dousing with flea powder is in order. Both of these items can be purchased at your pet shop.

A further preventive is a good aerosol flea and tick killer spray. When you use such preventives you should remember to change your Doberman's bedding, for fleas and lice like to let their eggs hatch in such places. It might not be a bad idea to sprinkle a little flea powder in your dog's sleeping area.

Facing page: *Intelligent and obedient, Doberman Pinschers must be favored subjects for formal dog portraits, such as this by Robert Pearcy.*

Remember, a little prevention goes a long way. If you can keep your dog free from fleas, you will also be protecting him from worms, since fleas are carriers of tapeworms.

Steps to take in the case of various injuries to your dog are similar to the principles of first aid for humans. You should carefully wash your dog's more superficial cuts and abrasions, and you should apply a disinfectant and a healing ointment. You might also apply a bandage to keep away dirt, but bandages are often hard to keep on dogs, as they sometimes chew them off. If a bandage is necessary, put a cardboard collar on your dog—then he won't be able to reach the bandage with his teeth. You can also tape your dog's nails, thus preventing scratching.

If you think your dog has a broken bone, don't move him until you have put a board splint on him.

If he is badly cut, you may need to apply a tourniquet. Apply it between the cut and the heart, and remember to loosen it every few minutes so that circulation will not be permanently damaged.

If you suspect your dog has swallowed poison, you might try to get him to vomit by giving him a solution of water, salt and mustard, but you certainly ought to rush him to the vet as soon as possible.

During hot weather, provide your dog with plenty of cool water. Also, never put him in a closed car that is standing in the sun. Certainly you know how hot such a place can be.

6.
General Care

One of the most convenient factors in owning a Doberman is that you do not have to spend much time grooming and cleaning him. He needs no hairclipping, little brushing, and few baths.

If needed, you can bathe your Doberman in the family bathtub. Photo by Vince Serbin.

It is impossible to predict when your Doberman will need a bath. He may remain perfectly clean for six months or he may get quite dirty in an hour. Therefore his bathing should depend upon his need.

Basically there are two ways to bathe your dog: you can give him a dry bath or you can give him a wet bath. For a wet bath you can purchase a dog soap or shampoo at your pet store. Unless otherwise instructed, fill a tub with warm water, put your dog in the tub, wet him down, and then rub him down with the soap or shampoo—and work up a good lather! But beware of getting soap or water into your dog's eyes and ears.

After soaping him down, rinse him off, being very careful to wash away any trace of the soap or shampoo (which might cause a skin irritation). Then dry him with a terry cloth towel and keep him in a warm, but not hot, place until he is thoroughly dried. Exercise after a bath is the best way to maintain his circulation. Beware of your dog's natural instinct to shake himself dry while you are bathing him, or you may end up as wet as he is.

Always use the right tool for clipping the nails of your Doberman. Under no circumstance should ordinary scissors be used. Photo by Vince Serbin.

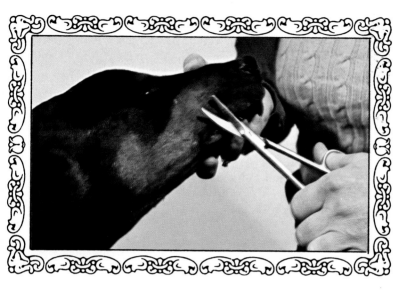

For a neater appearance, the stiff whiskers are cut close to the roots. It is simple and painless.

The advantage of a dry bath is—your dog doesn't get wet! This of course means he will be less susceptible to catching a cold. Again, your pet shop will have in stock various kinds of dry shampoos for dogs.

Each individual dry bath formula is different. Careful reading of the instructions appearing on the container is the first order before bathing. Usually, however, the mixture or shampoo is scrubbed into the coat. A thorough toweling completes the operation.

It is not necessary to brush your dog every day, but if you do he will have a healthier and shinier coat. Nonetheless, it can do no harm to establish regular brushing habits—then when your dog really needs a brushing he will not put up a fuss. Regular brushing will eliminate the necessity of frequent baths for your Dobe. Furthermore, it will help prevent his shedding throughout the house.

You will find that your pet does most of his shedding in the fall and in the spring, although a house pet will shed a little all year round. In times of heavy shedding, a brisk brushing will be necessary, for which will need a fairly stiff brush. Be firm but be gentle in brushing your Dobe, and if you accidentally hurt him a little, pat him and soothe him and you will find your pet will put up with the process of grooming.

Ear care

The ears of a dog are very sensitive and extreme care should be taken not to irritate them. Never wash out a dog's ear with soap and water. If it becomes necessary to clean the ear, swab it out with cotton and peroxide, or cotton with a little olive or sweet oil. Be gentle in this swabbing and do not probe deeper than you can see. A comercially prepared ear wash can be found at most pet shops and is usually quite effective.

Care of the teeth

Dogs that are allowed to gnaw on large bones, hard biscuits and rawhide bones or Nylabone® generally keep their teeth clean. Where discoloration shows, wipe teeth with hydrogen peroxide on a piece of cloth. Toothpaste also can be used.

Eyes, nose and nails

Generally your Dobe's eyes and nose will require no special care. One word of information regarding the nose—if your dog's nose is cold it is not necessarily an indication of good health. A cold nose simply means that your dog probably has no fever. And if your dog's nose is warm it is not necessarily an indication of a fever, for he may be in a warm house or a warm room.

If your Dobe's eyes are normal they will be bright and alert, and the eyelid will not cover any part of the eye. A bloodshot haw or a haw that partially covers the eye could be a sign of illness or some eye irritation. Perhaps your dog has little drops of pus in the corners of his eyes. Bathe with a soft, wet cloth.

Clip your Dobe's toenails with a pair of specially designed clippers weekly. When you are clipping his nails be careful not to cut into the "quick"—the vein of his nails. This could be painful for him. You can see where the quick is located, as it is of a whiter substance and it terminates in a sharp point an eighth of an inch or so before the end of the nail. Have someone of experience show you how to do this job before you try it yourself.

7.
Diseases

Home diagnosis of ailments among dogs is seldom dependable and often dangerous, although it is well for the owner to have as much knowledge as possible concerning what common symptoms of disorder might indicate. However, whenever possible, it is always best to consult a good veterinarian before administering any internal medicine.

A side benefit from training to retrieve is exercise that results from such activity. However, overactivity should be avoided, expecially in an immature Doberman. Photo by Sally Anne Thompson.

Loss of appetite may indicate any number of things. In many cases it simply indicates that your dog is not hungry for the moment. But if your dog refuses to eat for two consecutive days, then it is best to take him to your vet.

If your dog needs treatment for worms he will generally show one or more of the following symptoms: watery eyes, pus in inside corners of eyes, loose bowel movements, anemia, unthrifty coat, or loss of appetite.

If you find your dog frequently shaking his head, he may have something wrong with his ears which needs professional attention. A constant cough is a possible sign of illness. A runny nose may indicate no more than a slight cold, but if it is accompanied by a cough, a loss of appetite, or other such symptoms, you had better bring him to your vet for a checkup.

As you can see, the symptoms of dog diseases are not hard to spot, since they are not much different from the symptoms of human diseases. Common sense should tell you when to consult a professional.

Clean the ears regularly. Ear infections can be severe at times and can cause much pain. Photo by Sally Anne Thompson.

8.
Breeding

If you have a female and do not have her spayed you must be prepared for a female Doberman's heat period. It is during this period that your bitch should be mated, since you will have no success at any other time, but if you do not want her to have a litter of puppies, then you will have to keep a close watch over her in her heat period.

This Doberman bitch and puppy are owned by Fern Kowall of Scorpio Dobes, Finksburg, Md. Photo by Irene Weidler.

Your puppy's first period may occur at about seven months, but more normally it will occur at about nine months. From this time forth the period comes approximately once every six months and may last for up to four weeks.

In order to ascertain when she begins her heat period, watch for small droppings of blood and a swelling of her bottom. After the first week of the period the droppings take on a yellow stain, and the vulva (the bitch's external sex organ, her "bottom"), will be quite swollen. It is during this time (the second week) that she should be mated if mating is desired. During the third week the swelling subsides and the droppings cease.

It is usually not wise to have your puppy bred during her first heat period. Remember also—whenever you do not want your bitch to produce a litter, keep her shut indoors! Provide her with a make-shift toilet such as papers or a special area and take her outside for regular walks on a leash. If you want to keep the neighborhood dogs away from your doorstep during this period (which is not an easy task!) take her some distance away from your house to excrete.

Two Dobes enjoying their leisure time chewing Nylabones.

Examine the teeth and mouth of your Doberman at regular intervals. Photo by Sally Anne Thompson.

If you want to have her spayed, consult your vet for advice. It is probably best to have her spayed *after* she is at least six months old.

Most breeders generally mate their Dobes on about the 12th or 14th day of "season," which is just after the preliminary vaginal discharge has stopped.

Before breeding her she should be wormed thoroughly and given a complete checkup by a competent veterinarian. The major reason for this is to protect the litter, although, of course, no female Dobe should be bred while she is in a rundown condition.

Your dog's period of gestation will run from 58 to 65 days, with the average 62 or 63 days, approximately nine weeks. During this time, the diet of the matron is of much importance. It must be of sufficient quantity and quality to maintain the matron herself and bring about the development of her family in embryo. It should contain the vitamins, carbohydrates, fats, proteins, and minerals necessary. Whole milk and egg yolk should be given along with cereal in the morning. To her evening meal of prepared food, horse-meat or lean beef, canned slamon and liver should be added fre-

47

A beautiful head study of a Doberman Pinscher. Note his alert appearance and proud posture. Photo by Sally Anne Thompson.

quently. For two weeks before whelping, her diet should contain less bulk and more concentrated food—more meat, raw or cooked, should be given and her milk ration increased.

Exercise is important. This should be mild but regular. As she grows heavy in whelp, she will be inclined to remain idle but should be taken for regular short walks on the leash.

After about five weeks you will want to introduce your Dobe to her whelping box. This should consist of a wooden floor with sides but no top. A rail a few inches off the floor is advisable so that she cannot crowd the puppies against the sides of the box. Several layers of newspapers may serve as bedding.

She should be disturbed as little as possible but watched carefully during whelping. After the first expulsive effort is seen, it is safe to allow one hour before the first delivery. However, if the straining is severe and the hour passes without results, the attention of a competent veterinarian should be sought immediately.

Weaning

Efforts to wean the puppies should start when they are about four weeks old. The mother will generally start this procedure herself.

For the first meal place the following mixture in a shallow dish:
>One cup warm milk,
>one yolk of egg
>one teaspoonful Karo syrup,
>one teaspoonful lime water.

The puppies' heads should be repeatedly dipped into the dish until they begin to lap the mixture voluntarily. They learn quickly, and are cute as can be when they catch on.

In a very short time they will be eagerly taking four such meals a day. The amount of milk should then be doubled, and one or two thin pieces of dry toast, crumbled, can be added. At five weeks of age some Pablum or pre-cooked cereal can be added. At this time the mother is separated from her litter and is returned only for short nursing periods.

By the time the puppies are eight weeks of age a good daily diet is as follows:

MORNING: Milk, dry cereal or oatmeal, one tablespoonful lime water, one teaspoonful Karo syrup.

NOON: Chopped raw or cooked beef, well-cooked mashed carrots or spinach, prepared puppy meal. Cod-liver oil.

ABOUT 4 P.M.: Beef or mutton broth mixed with rice or barley, with cooked tomatoes sometimes added, seasoned with salt.

ABOUT 8 P.M.: Milk and toast or cereal, one tablespoonful lime water, one teaspoonful Karo syrup.

This young Doberman has yet to sit straight. This will come naturally as he grows older. Photo by Sally Anne Thompson.

9.
Training

Your Doberman is an alert, intelligent dog and will make a willing pupil. But you must be willing to spend time with your pet if you wish him to grow into an obedient, well-trained adult.

Do not be discouraged if your Doberman resists obeying your command. Photo by Vince Serbin.

There are two vital rules that you must follow in any training procedure: (1) be consistent; and (2) be patient. Your Doberman will try to understand and please you. Nevertheless, you will have to go through the training steps again and again until he learns the desired response and can give it on command. Be firm with your dog, but kind to him; be strict but gentle. When you have a command, use the shortest phrase possible—"Sit" rather than "Sit down" or "Stay" rather than "Stay there."

Use your command to mean the same thing at all times. Your dog learns by associating the sound and intonation of the command with his training and response as he has been taught.

Collar and leash training

By the time your pup is five months old he should be pretty well housebroken. Now you can start more complicated aspects of his education.

Many Doberman Pinscher owners prefer the choke chain collar for both young and adult dogs. Photo by Sally Anne Thompson.

52

A handler holding the head to show the length of the neck for judging. Photo by Sally Anne Thompson.

Although your pet will probably not need a license until he is six months old, he should become used to a collar at an earlier age. You must be sure that he will not struggle out of his collar while he is outside playing, especially if you are not with him.

Buy your young Doberman a collar as soon as you bring him home. Get an inexpensive leather collar at first. Just as children outgrow their clothes, puppies outgrow their collars several times before they reach full size.

Let your pup wear his collar around the house until he becomes used to the feel of it. This should not take more than a few days. When he no longer is uncomfortable, you may fasten on the leash.

The first few times you attach the leash to his collar, just let the pup pull it around after him. Always watch to be sure that he doesn't chew the leash. In the second week you should try to lead him. Your puppy will resist. He may balk, pull, or sit down and simply refuse to budge. Coax him to follow while maintaining a firm pull on the leash.

Allow about ten minutes each day for leash training. Your pet's period of concentration is short, and a longer session will bore and tire him. Before long, he will learn that the pull of the leash must be obeyed, and presto!—he will walk along at your side as nicely as can be. But remember—this result cannot be attained in a day. You must be patient and constant, using love and praise rather than punishment.

Let's learn to walk

Now your puppy has learned to respect the restraints of collar and leash. The next step is to teach him to walk at your left side, while you hold the handle of the leash in your right hand, letting it cross in front of you. This arrangement gives you the greatest control over your dog in any situation. The slack is held loosely in your left hand.

If your dog starts to pull in one direction, simply stop walking and jerk the leash gently but firmly with your left hand. Remain at a standstill for several minutes; then continue the walk. If he again starts to pull, repeat your tactics. When your pup learns that he must behave properly to go out with you at all, and that he actually has a great deal of freedom within the confines of his lead, your tribulations are over. You and your pet can now walk comfortably together. You will never find yourself flying helplessly along at the end of a leash while your powerful, stately Doberman terrorizes the neighborhood cats.

Sit: Take your dog for his daily walks. Now, as he is standing next to you on loose lead, push his hindquarters down gently and give the new command, "Sit". You may have to hold the leash high with your right hand to prevent him from lying all the way down. When your pup is in the "Sit" position, pat him and fuss over him. Then give the command to "Come", walk a few steps, and repeat the "Sit" lesson. When your dog has mastered the "Sit" routine while on his leash, use the same method to teach him without it.

Stay: "Stay" is an invaluable lesson in your Doberman's training. You may want him to remain in the car while you are shopping, to stay in the kitchen while you answer the front door, or to be quiet when friends drop over.

Once your Doberman has learned to "Come" and to "Sit," teaching him to "Stay" is not at all difficult. First, command him to "Sit" position. Drop the leash and back four or five paces away from him, facing him as you do this. Command him to "Stay". If he rises to follow you, walk quickly back to the pup, push him firmly into the "Sit" position, and go through the whole process again. Repeat the lesson until he remains where he is even when you walk completely out of his sight.

When you want your pet to break the "Stay", tell him to "Come." NEVER let him break before you call him, but be sure you don't forget to call him when you do want him to rise.

Some don'ts for your Dobe

Most people want to teach their dog three strict "don'ts": don't jump on people, don't get on the furniture, and don't bark. A dog who has one or more of these bad habits can be a terrible nuisance to his own family.

Your dog should be trained not to bark without just cause. Every time he barks at a friend or a delivery man, give him the sharp command "QUIET!" If this does not work you may have to resort to the newspaper method—but never swat your dog! Take the newspaper and swat your own hand in order to make a loud cracking noise, then firmly voice the command "QUIET!" This seldom fails to be effective. But you must be persistent—if you let your dog get away with even a single bark it will be that much more difficult to train him.

There is hardly a puppy or a young dog in existence which never has the strong urge to exuberantly display his affection by jumping on a person. No doubt your Dobe has shown his devotion in this unpleasant manner, and perhaps you have not known just how to stop it. If your dog has already learned the command "Sit" or "Down," then you will have no problem—simply give the command in a firm, authoritative voice. If he has not yet learned one of these commands, you can take the direct course of action of merely bending your knee so that your dog's chest will bump into it when he jumps, thus teaching him that it is rather impractical to jump on people.

55

It will not be an easy task to train your Dobe to stay off the furniture. Furniture is very comfortable, and besides, it has the pleasant odor of the people whom your Dobe loves! Your Dobe's nose is quite remarkable—it can smell things that no human nose can. Thus it is possible to combat your dog's tendency to get on the furniture by soaking a small rag with a special scent repulsive to dogs but odorless to humans. Place this rag on any piece of furniture your Dobe likes, and he will soon change his opinion. The great advantage of the "scented rag" technique is that you don't have to watch your dog every minute of the day. Dog-repellent sprays are available at your pet shop.

Training for the show ring

If you bought your dog without intending to show him, the chances are that you do not have a champion. Professional breeders will keep the pups whose pedigrees are well stocked with champion ancestors—or they will sell them at quite high prices. Nonetheless, it is not the pedigree that is judged in the show ring—and it is certainly possible that you may have a winner.

In training the dog for the show ring, a number of things must be considered. The dog must be constantly alert to his handler and practically oblivious to his surroundings. He must travel free and easily, with natural carriage, whether the leash be short or long. He must move willingly and freely with his handler in any direction. He must stand quietly in any position in which his handler cares to pose him, remaining motionless until allowed to relax. He must stand quietly and willingly for examination, allowing a stranger, the judge, to examine him minutely, going over him thoroughly with his hands. And he must keep an even temper at all times.

The first lesson should be lead-breaking and should be continued throughout the dog's career. Not only can the dog be taught that he must remain under control at all times in this manner, but much good exercise can be secured by pacing him. With the lead held short, cause the dog to walk close to your side for several yards at a time. Then have him run close to your side. Keep this up until he comes along readily and naturally. Then slacken your hold on the lead and have him come along with you, slow and then at quickened pace. Keep him traveling in a straight line, jerking him lightly if he tries to waver. Have him circle when you stop, turning clockwise. These lessons are not difficult, for the dog soon catches on to what you want him to do. They should be practiced every day. Do not allow him to pull you. He is to follow where you lead. Reward him frequently when he does well.

In teaching your dog to pose, step in front or to the side of the dog with the lead slack. Attract his attention with a tidbit or toy until he moves into the stance you desire. Set his forelegs so that they are parallel, then move his hind legs into proper position. Teach him to stand quietly with all four legs squarely under him. Have him remain standing in this position for several minutes at a time, talking to him in low tones occasionally and running your hand along his back and neck. This will require patience on your part,but with careful handling your efforts will be rewarded. Your task is to have him let you pose him as you desire and remain standing in that position until you allow him to change it. Keep his head up and alert, his ears where they should be, and his position such as to show his good points. The judge can only form his opinion of what he sees.

In posing the dog, place your left arm over the dog's back and, with your right hand between his front legs at the brisket, lift him slightly and set his front legs parallel to each other and at right angles to the floor. It may be necessary for you to set each leg separately. See that he is well up on his toes. See that his elbows are where they should be.

Now place his hind legs properly, so that the weight of the body is evenly distributed on all four feet. Study the standard of the breed carefully and have your dog's pose conform to it as much as possible.

With the muzzle parallel with the floor, hold the dog's head out with the right hand, so that all the length of neck is shown. With your left hand hold his tail in proper position.

After the dog learns to pose easily and quietly, have some friend, a stranger to the dog, act as a "judge" and go over the dog. Get him thoroughly accustomed to this sort of handling by using several friends at various times. Then practice by posing him with other dogs, simulating show ring conditions as much as possible.

If the dog is inclined to be self-conscious or timid, take him with you everywhere you can, in stores, in crowds, etc., until he has lost his fear of strange surroundings and strange people.

Study your own dog's conformation. Compare his measurements and weight with those of the standard. If he's too light try to put more flesh on him, if he's too heavy take it off. Spend as much time as possible with your dog, leading him, handling him, posing him. He'll pay you in the show ring for your trouble.

Never be hasty with him, and never become excited. Talk to him occasionally in calm, low tones and reward him frequently with caresses and small morsels. If he is possessed of the proper show ring temperament, he will respond readily.

Allowing your Doberman Pinscher to get on the furniture is a personal matter. He can be trained not to do so, if you wish. Photo by Diane McCarthy.

10.
Showing

After you have carefully trained your Dobe for the ring, and after you have gained some experience in a local show or two, you will be ready for the larger, "point" show. The smaller show judges the males and females of the breed together. The larger show judges the male, the female, and each breed separately, and also gives an

Terry Lazzaro, handler, with a Doberman of show quality, as can be judged by his appearance and stance. Photo by Vince Serbin.

award for best in show. The reason the larger shows are called "point" shows is that under certain conditions a dog can win points towards its championship at such shows—when a dog has accumulated a certain number of qualifying points it becomes a champion. For these larger shows, entries close several weeks in advance. To obtain information regarding the time and locations of shows in your locality, write to your national registry association. In the United States, for example, you'd write to the American Kennel Club (51 Madison Ave., New York NY 10010) and in Great Britain to The Kennel Club of Great Britain, 1 Clarges St., Piccadilly, London W1Y 8AB). The following comments about shows are based on American dog show practices; they can of course vary from place to place.

A large dog show is quite a production. Hundreds of dogs come from every reach of the vicinity—perhaps some are even imported from other cities—to be judged. Dog stalls will be lined up and down the sides of the building, and your dog will have been assigned one of them. It is a strange and dizzying spectacle to the newcomer, and so you will need to prepare a show kit to make things as easily as possible.

Included in this show kit should be a water dish, a bottle of water, a chain or a leash, a show lead, grooming tools, and your identification ticket. The reason for the water dish is obvious—but why the bottled water? For one, it is not wise to take chances with a strange source of water in a public place—you never know what diseases may be passed around among the numerous dogs. Secondly, it simply is a bother to go looking for a place for your dog to get a drink.

You will need a short chain leash to fasten your Dobe to the stall where he is to stay during the show (except, of course, while he himself is being shown). The show lead is a thin leash and collar combination which adds to the appearance as much as does the regular collar and leash.

The day before the show, groom your dog thoroughly—this will remove loose hairs and dust and will make his coat gleam. You should also cut his toenails and clip his whiskers close to his muzzle, and his eyebrows should also be closely clipped. This will give his face a smooth appearance. Give your dog only a light meal the morning of the show. He will "show" more enthusiastically.

When you arrive at the show the official veterinarian will give your dog a general health checkup. Then you should find the dog's place and make him comfortable there.

Before his class is called, take your Dobe to the exercise ring to relieve himself. Give him a final grooming, and take your place at the ring to wait for the class.

The winners from each class compete against each other for Winner's Dog. The Doberman chosen from this group then competes against the best female, next against champions from "specials" classes. The winner here is "Best Doberman" and must now compete against other breeds—Boxers, Collies—in the Working Group. Finally, the emergent victor competes against the Sporting, Hound, Terrier, Non-Sporting, Herding, and Toy winners for Best in Show.

Here's to Dobes and their owners!

You are now one of the select few—one of the special set—and as long as you remain a Dobe owner you will maintain this distinction. For the Doberman is a special dog, and it takes a special person to own one.

You will find that your Doberman is more valuable to you than you ever imagined—for his vital spirit, his marvelous affection, his huge heart and ever-growing friendship will be mysteriously and astronomically compounded in the reflection of your sentiments.

You will find endless hours of pleasure watching your Doberman puppy scamper awkwardly toward a graceful adulthood. You will thoroughly enjoy teaching him commands and tricks, giving him new toys, and, perhaps, showing him.

So here's to Dobes and their owners!